LEAFMEAL

South African, English & Canadian Poems
(1957–2007)

Alan Bishop

Rock's Mills Press
Oakville, Ontario

For Judith, Matthew, Ann & Ruth,
with my love;
for my friends Eric, Ron & Neville;
& in memory of my Mother & Father,
& Professors Oosthuizen & Butler

Published by
Rock's Mills Press
www.rocksmillspress.com

Copyright © 2021, 2020 by Alan Bishop
All rights reserved. Published by arrangement with the author.

First printing: 2020
Second printing, with revisions and corrections: 2021

No part of this book may be used, reproduced, stored in or introduced into a retrieval system, or transmitted in any form or by any means (electronic, mechanical, photocopying, recording or otherwise) without the prior consent in writing of the publisher.

Spring and Fall:
to a young child

Margaret, are you grieving
Over Goldengrove unleaving?
Leaves, like the things of man, you
With your fresh thoughts care for, can you?
Ah! as the heart grows older
It will come to such thoughts colder
By and by, nor spare a sigh
Though worlds of wanwood leafmeal lie;
And yet you will weep and know why.
Now no matter, child, the name:
Sorrow's springs are the same.
Nor mouth had, no nor mind, expressed
What heart heard of, ghost guessed:
It is the blight man was born for,
It is Margaret you mourn for.

Gerard Manley Hopkins (1844–89)

Three lives hath one life -
Iron, honey, gold.

"August 1914", Isaac Rosenberg

And where you are is where you are not.
"East Coker", *Four Quartets*, T.S.Eliot

Contents

Preface ... 7

fir in winter ... 9

South African Poems, 1957–1960
    Contemporaneous Impressions ... 13
    'Before the axe descends' ... 14
    Warnings ... 15
    A South African Epitaph ... 16
    White South Africa ... 17
    Waiters ... 18
    Joseph Ndalo ... 19
    After Sharpeville: Grahamstown, May 1960 ... 20
    How it is ... 21
    Tiger, tiger ... 22
    on the beach ... 23
    Sonnet on my 23rd Birthday, August 1960 ... 24

English Poems, 1961–1969
    Search ... 27
    In the torture ... 28
    Nightmare ... 29
    ballad for James Joyce ... 30
    Charlotte Bronte ... 31
    Q. ... 32
    Gamut ... 33
    Winter/Spring ... 34
    Love ... 35

Canadian Poems, 1970–2007
    Another Immigrant ... 39
    For John Thompson ... 40

Two Trivial Poems ... 41
Pelicans ... 42
Behind the Wire ... 44
Concatenation: an Elegy ... 46
Why Trees? ... 51
Words, words ... 52

The Golden Spruce ... 55

Preface

These are occasional poems of an occasional poet, composed over some fifty years. They are very diverse in theme, tone, length and especially form; written at different times in different places.

Looking through my mess of old poems recently, I found some that seemed worth preserving. They were written in three countries during three periods of my life – some in circumstances now unfamiliar, so that their meaning is to some extent dependent upon, or enhanced by, contextual information. Hence this Preface.

The two poems that frame this selection are concrete poems, & in both a tree is the poem's symbolic centre; their theme being heroism. The first, "fir in winter", expressed, in about 1960, my admiration for three heroes of the anti-apartheid struggle in South Africa: Nelson Mandela (then still at liberty but threatened with imprisonment), Alan Paton (author of *Cry, the Beloved Country*), & Trevor Huddleston, CR (author of *Naught for your Comfort*). In their brave ability to stand firm despite contumely, they seemed to me like great evergreens among lesser, deciduous trees. The final poem in this selection, written nearly a half-century later, takes its title from a book by John Vaillant which narrates the story of a contemporary Canadian hero, Grant Hadwin, who protested against deforestation on the Canadian West Coast. Between those two 'tree-poems', the text is divided into into three sections, by chronology & place of composition.

From 1957 to 1960, I was an undergraduate at Rhodes University in South Africa. "Contemporaneous Impressions" won a University prize. "Warnings" is primarily a response to the then-fear of nuclear conflict between the USA & Russia. But most of the poems in this section relate to political unrest in South Africa, as the apartheid system was increasingly challenged, with protests being disrupted by harsh Police action. Rhodes University was under surveillance – my Philosophy Professor, Dr D.C.S. Oosthuizen, was 'banned' & sentenced to house-arrest; & like many of my fellow-students, I participated in protest-marches & had my name recorded by the Police as a trouble-maker. 'Coloureds' (South African of mixed race) were trapped in the racial divide, vulnerable to rejection by both Blacks & Whites; I came to know an elderly woman, a cleaner in my University Residence, & attended her funeral when she died suddenly ("A South African Epitaph"). "White South Africa" focuses on the self-destructive reluctance of Whites to initiate social & political changes needed to avert the violence they feared. "Waiters" is based on my frequent evening experience, before Dinner in the nearby dining-hall, of hearing two Waiters conversing in their vernacular, as they relaxed on the lawn just below the window of my Residence room. "Joseph Ndalo" is a deliberately-simple account of the aftermath of a Police shooting, at the time of the Sharpeville Massacre, in which sixty-nine Black civilians were killed. "After Sharpeville" records my sombre thoughts as I saw sunset darkening the late afternoon while the military band of a nearby White school marched noisily into what seemed likely to be a very bleak future.

The 'English' poems of the second section were all written while I read English at Corpus Christi, Oxford, during the early 1960s. The occasions that provoked them, as well as the poems themselves, need no explication. While still much concerned with death & suffering, these poems now suggest to me some relaxation, after the tensions of life in apartheid South Africa.

After three years in Oxford, I returned to my native Zimbabwe (then still Rhodesia); taught for a year (1965) at a Black high-school; married; & then accepted a lectureship in the Department of English Language at the University of Cape Town – just before UDI (Ian Smith's Unilateral Declaration of Independence: an attempt to preserve White control that precipitated a tragic fifteen-year civil war). Our time in Cape Town ended aburptly, within a year, when the Government, taking measures against anti-apartheid university-teachers, expelled us. I returned to Oxford, completed a D.Phil within two years, then we emigrated to Canada (which I had visited in 1964 & whose Prime Minister, Lester Pearson, we admired for his stand against apartheid). During that fraught five-year period, I wrote little poetry.

Settling into a more stable life in Ontario (after a year at Mount Allison University, New Brunswick, which gave me a brief friendship with the poet John Thompson, whose sadly early death inspired a poem using the ghazals form of his final book, *Stilt Jack*), I began to find some time & inclination for writing poetry. "Behind the Wire" responded to a fine etching by George Wallace, a Professor of Fine Arts at McMaster University; when, in 1977, he gave our Amnesty International group free fund-raising use of that etching, it led me into a meditation on cruelty & suffering which included reference to Nelson Mandela, then imprisoned on Robben Island, near Cape Town. The longest of the 'Canadian' poems, "Concatenation: an Elegy", is also the most ambitious poem I have written. Two deaths inaugurated it: I received a letter telling me that Anthea Joseph had died (widow of Michael Joseph, she had inherited his role as publisher of novels by Joyce Cary, some of whose writings I had edited); that same day, I had come across a run-over cat dying at the roadside, telephoned the SPCA from a nearby public telephone, & waited, helpless to alleviate the animal's agony. And finally, "Pelicans": I hesitated to include this ugly, angry poem; but have come to feel that, of all my poems, it may be the best – certainly it goes on mattering deeply to me.

ALAN BISHOP

fir
in winter

who nobly so lofty stands leaved
(left a texture of leaf
moving) unmoved
clothed among nude
trees

who lonely so lovely stands grieved
(in simple agony of grief
moving) unmoved
clothed among nude
trees

who nobly so lofty stands leaved
who lonely so lovely stands grieved

stands

(among trees)

South African Poems

1957–1960

Contemporaneous Impressions

"A child who with its eyes bandaged had lost several of his fingers by amputation, continued to complain for many days successively of pains, now in this joint and now in that, of the very fingers that had been cut off. Des Cartes was led by this incident to reflect on the uncertainty with which we attribute any particular place to any inward pain or uneasiness, and proceeded after long consideration to establish it as a general law; that contemporaneous impressions, whether images or sensations, recall each other mechanically." (Coleridge, *Biographia Literaria*, Chapter V)

I

O it was ecstasy of agony and way
beyond your understanding, child:
rolling breakers of pain piled
upon beaches of sanded nerve
in the sweep of the, curve
of the, body's bay.

And the twist, O the twist
of those phantom fingers
forming a phantom fist
to strike at, to break,
that cruel love,
that loving hate.

II

But the sober mind observes;
noting each start and each spasm
of the abstract organism;
each scream of its knackered nerves.

And a theory revolves into being
in the still small space of the skull:
thrust of a pitiless brain,
a child's pain.

Before the axe descends
and blood proclaims a birth,
no beginnings and no ends
ungreen the green of earth.

All's one, continuous
 as the muscled lift and sweep,
the gradual fall upon us,
the shining axe of sleep.

Warnings

Children will touch our skulls
among the piles of dusty bones
gently and with awe,
wondering what this jones
or smith saw
that made him stare at the white sky
and drop his jaw
to scream or grin and die.

But soon again their joyful yells
will clutch the silence, when they play
with heads of men who once were tall
and splendidly built.

We played ball
too, were often gay
in spite of our guilt.

A South African Epitaph

The funeral was held on a dreary day.
The Lord must have thought it better that way,
in order to save us excessive strain:
it's easier to mourn in the wind and the rain
      than it is to be sad in the sun.

She'd been something to us, we two that were there –
not much, but something. So we clench and stare,
and try our best to act some grief
to a gallery of trees, whose quivering leaf
      laughs at our wintry deceit.

She died at a most inconvenient time,
not thinking of us, or how we should climb
that weary hill with her coffin between us,
hoping that none of our friends had seen us,
      and wishing the rain would stop.

She wasn't the kind – you know what I mean –
with whom one normally likes to be seen.
She was old and ugly, her skin dark brown,
and she lived in the poorest part of the town:
      death couldn't alter that.

I feel we've been trapped by a sense of duty,
and sombrely pity myself. The beauty
of surging poplars endorses my claim
that I've been hard done by. At last we came
      to the edge of the open grave.

As I stand there, I try to recall her face,
its lace of wrinkles, the sudden grace
when she smiled at me. But the image went blank,
so I stared at my feet as the coffin sank
      and slowly drifted from view.

The priest concluded his gabble and went,
leaving us soaked in the rain. I bent
to look into her grave. He touched my elbow:
"Thank God that's over. Come on, let's go."
      We left her there, alone.

White South Africa

Here we lie in the gentle sun
  close to a seething sea
and all our work is undone, undone
  for warm in the sun are we

While we lie dreaming all day, all day
  close to a seething sea
men and women shall pass away
  for warm in the sun are we

Never a move or sound we make
  close to a seething sea
never again to wake, to wake
  for warm in the sun are we

And when the long night comes, o comes
  close to a seething sea
we shall not hear the beat of drums
  for warm in the sun are we

We will not hear the drums, the drums
  through all eternity

Waiters

Patiently they sit below my window,
surveying this dying day:
two Waiters, waiting for Dinner to summon,
waiting to serve – impassive in the long, polished Hall –
us pink and noisy adjuncts of their servile state,
while the slow hot shadows lengthen.

Patiently they sit below my window,
unmoving – bowed heads, dark arms and hands –
and one is straight-backed, young; the other bent
towards his grave – and both wear white aprons.

Two Waiters, waiting –
                    Their faces, their faces?
            I cannot see their faces from my window
              and I wonder if their gaze is still
                    calm and patient, for a
                        changing wind
                      has whipped the
                          trees to madness, and a chill
                          splits the
                              afternoon.

Joseph Ndalo

Joseph Ndalo's mother was shot
where dust arose and the sun was hot.
She happened to stand on the edge of a crowd
when "Fire!" the Sergeant cried aloud.

He swore in the Court he hadn't said it.
Because he was White they gave him credit
and let him off with a reprimand.
His men stood him beers all round.

The Blacks were frightened to tell their story –
it made the incident seem more gory.
As they stood in the murmuring Court
sober faces masked their thought.

The Judge expressed sincere regret
and urged that all should forgive and forget.
But that didn't give a home and bread
to Joseph Ndalo, whose mother is dead.

After Sharpeville: Grahamstown, May 1960

Beaten to dust by drums
                    and bugles, the sun dissolves.
This jewelled city hums.
                    Now words are worlds that revolve
on the mind's axis, slanted
in silence. Slowly, evening comes.

                    Weave your wistful dream
in lovely light, enchanted.
                    Peace and joy shall seem
alive, death supplanted
                    by sleep. Now time
                    slows in the sun's last gleam.

But then the march of the school
                    cadets – those bugles that climb
in shrieks to the sky, that cruel
                    rattle of drums – reminds
me of this day's despair. Night
will drain that sunset's bloodied pool.

How it is

On Monday, today's newspaper says, fifteen men will die,
all of them Black. Ask why,
there's an answer: some killed,
others raped or robbed. Dangerous men,
unfit to live. Their bodies must be stilled,
their souls (if they have souls) flung
to eternal darkness. Then?
Some friends and relatives may mourn their being hung.

But on Monday morning I'll be swotting
(I haven't killed, raped or robbed, and my exam is near)
while their bodies plunge and jerk and begin rotting.
What have I to do with their pain, their fear?

Tiger, tiger

This fierce beast wakes again,
and stalks the borders of its cage.
Moved by some paroxysm of rage,
it claws and roars.
(They call this beast dumb
that implores
its keeper for freedom?)
And shall I set it free?
(I that require other men
to keep their animals under lock and key.)
As it rises in shining beauty,
leaps with graceful ease,
no concept of duty
could seize
my hands from the door of its cage.
Merely to see
such glory is to love such rage.
(And which is beast, which me?)

on the beach

change of weather comes too fast
catching us unawares
in the midst of urgent vast
concern with stares

that must we move from heavy heat
of angry sun
to terrors of shade (a sheet
conceals the one

of bedded bodies wild in lust)
for men must seek
the huge of heat (from dust
in a short leak

    of life to dust we move) each crust
    (as urgently we touch)
    scatters and scatters and scatters to *must*

(this beach is such
a harsh place) don't move
away (no matter how much
the wind lifts the sand my love

into your eyes)
lets burn from *be* to *not*
dissolve eternities
of *never* to *always* (oh forgot

our concern with stares)
lie cracked together in sand
oozing unawares
each *must* and *must* and *must* to *and*

Sonnet on my 23rd birthday, August 1960

Like any other day: I sit or stand;
decide to write a letter, don't; lie
on my bed and listen to radio Bach; sigh
at thoughts of work undone; and have I planned
that meeting for tomorrow, and did I land
that interview? And so the sun slips by
my pettiness, and one day I will die,
and here's my life pouring through the years like sand.

So little of worth in twenty-two years!
So much waste, futility, hesitation;
opportunities unseen, ignored – a few taken.
Yet: alive! No cause, no cause for tears.
Existence: ecstasy. Afire in the fire of creation –
shaken by earth and sea and sky - shaken - shaken …

English Poems

1961–1969

Search

We went looking for bones on the hillside:
lifted the dank leaves to poke at sullen earth:
and found none.

The boy said, pluming greyness:
"So many things die and we never know."

Mist came, and a long stillness.
At the centre of my body, bones.

In the torture

chamber of Warwick Castle,
I saw, beyond the rack,
a thumbscrew
dainty as milady's necklace,
its maker's initials engraved
and a filigree flourish.
Monstrous, someone said,
to actually take pride in *that*;
But I thought, How very
human.

In the dungeon,
my shadow stains the wall,
my breath susurrates
above the oubliette.

Outside, in the rain,
a peacock shrieks at
me.

Nightmare

As I turned the corner and crossed the street,
I heard the sound of running feet.

As I crossed the street and entered a shop,
I heard the footsteps abruptly stop.

As I entered the shop and bought some gin,
I heard a creak as the feet came in.

As I bought some gin and left in a hurry,
I heard the footsteps behind me scurry.

As I left in a hurry and started to run,
I heard them follow me one by one.

As I started to run and stopped again,
I heard the footsteps enter my brain.

As I stopped again and turned in terror,

ballad for james joyce

to the auriculate jungle
of our vocabulary
he took his machete
and swore he would cut down the tree

tigers of nouns roared
pronominal cubs purred
but he lifted his machete
as if he hadn't heard

parrots of verbs flew
screaming the air to flame
but he lifted his machete
and prepared to take aim

snakes of adjectives hissed
adverbial monkeys swang
but he lifted his machete
and through the air it sang

a pigmy preposition
shot a conjunctive dart
but he lifted his machete
and cleaved the tree apart

now lets praise this gallant hunter
with noises wild and free
for with his machete
he cut down the grammar tree

Charlotte Bronte

And she remained
last rock athwart the current
to marry
and to suffer and to die

The moor
beat hard upon the graveyard
and a chill
held watch about their walls

One seeks a totem

They wrote

They were

They are

Q.

William, I would like to ask you what,

our birth being "but a sleep and a forgetting",

our death is not?

Gamut

A Song of Death

Have you heard that I am dead?
I died last night, you know –
suddenly got it into my head
        it was time to go.

Held my breath till I burst;
fell down, heavy, cold.
No more hunger, no more thirst!
        And I won't grow old.

I sleep on a cloud of dreams;
joy laves warm about me.
Never wake up again, it seems!
        Do without me.

A Song of Life

Pack up all your dreams:
you've a long way to go.
In dirty hotel rooms
you'll need a warming glow.

Dreams are fragile things
and burn in easy fires.
Don't borrow any matches –
use up your desires.

The journey's very tiring
and maybe has no end.
Pack up all your dreams –
you have no choice, my friend.

Winter/Spring

This gaunt black tree, his spindly limbs caressed
by glistening snow, considers the moon;
cold she is, darkly yearns for rest.
His fingers implore: when will it thaw? - Soon.

Wet wind shivers; illegible sky sows
a scatter of snowflakes across the moon.
A swan slides on its hungry shadow, goes.
Turning earth, travail of birth? - Soon.

Interstice of space and time: seething seeds
glitter from flake to flake, and the moon
sighs, sighs and droops. Winter bleeds.
Dawn will sing the song of spring? - Soon

Love

You will never know
how much my fingers feel
your presence.
Just so, just so,
I touch the essence
of this cloth. Not real

is the you I see
across the silent hall,
staring?
Sensibility
your tender caring
gave me: power to call

your image close. So:
I watch, feeling the dress
you stroke.
You'll never know.
But if I spoke,
I think – I think you'd guess.

Canadian Poems

1970–2007

Another Immigrant

I have found what I may
have been looking for in
Canada. This air-conditioned exile.
Less frequent occasions for the grosser sin.
I charm more easily here, am easily benevolent. Nothing is deep
or of necessary seriousness. There is always time to pay.
Shall I put it like this. I smile.
Those other I's can weep.

For John Thompson:

Ghazals on Learning of the Death of a Canadian Poet

Beyond the flesh, too, we reach
and touch, perhaps.

I hardly knew you then. Yet now
recall a snow-filled night nine years ago -

the way you left that darkened whiteness,
came into the low cave of our warmth -

how we two sat, late, late: beers, chat,
and the black strangeness of your agony -

those polar silences, chasms where we hurtled, flailed -
how we crawled like broken bears back to life -

you twist your empty beer-glass between your knees
and your eyes turning to me, turning - and I

ask now, too late - turn too
and across your crazy loss

ask why, how, why -
knowing nothing too, John.

Friend? Words for you.

Two Trivial Poems

For a University Administrator

How does one communicate with

>5 monkeys up a tree
>Gloria Swanson
>extra-terrestrial bodies
>the Canadian Constitution
>published academics in decline
>lovers in the act
>speakers of *Proto-Indo-European
>the dead

Snow

Doors and floors squeak.
Mice as they scurry for safety squeak.

Lazy lovers may sometimes squeak.
Show-girls and Marilyn Monroe in *Some Like it Hot* squeak.

A short or slight sound of a high-pitched character is a squeak.

He had a narrow squeak.
Pips squeak.

>The snow under my boots
>squeaks.

Pelicans

*We sup full with horrors every day
and are never satiated*

In today's paper, a photo of
a young man in Brazil jumping
from a great height, jumping
to his death, to splattered flesh
on stones or concrete –
and the watching crowd
(or so the caption says)
yelled "Jump! Jump! Jump! Jump!"

> *feed us, die to feed us with
> your body*

And my mind still retches, flinches
from the article about
a South African woman battered
to death, her spread vagina
stuffed with glass –
and the watching crowd
screaming hatred, "Traitor! Traitor! Traitor! Traitor!"
(and someone took a photo)

> *and die, feed us, die to feed us with
> your blood*

                        What are we
                        What are we
                        What are we
        What are we What are we What are we
        What are we What are we What are we
        What are we What are we What are we
                        What are we
                        What are we
                        What are we
                        What are we
                        What are we
                        What are we
                        What are we
                        What are we
                        What are we
                        What are we

The animals turn their
eyes away and
ponder silence while we
slit their throats for
breakfast, while we
boil their brains for
tea, while we
                eat
                        them

A little water
clears us of
                Body

Who would have
thought the old man
                Blood

All the perfumes of Arabia,
all great Neptune's ocean

Behind the Wire

Smiling sadly out of the dusk
of his suffering,

Elderly Jew of Auschwitz:
watchmaker by trade;
lost all his hair after they
took his wife and three daughters
to another camp; his glasses,
gold-rimmed, for safety
confiscated by the kindest guard;
blinking, smiling shyly, sadly,
shuffles to the wire –
habits of benignity die hard.
He has gold teeth too.

Argentinian widow:
you jug-eared whore,
here, come here, you
ask what happened
to your son Jorge who
had no politics, he was good,
"a good doctor, a good man,
helping all others" –
here, closer, Mother,
bring your shaved head
closer to the wire, closer, closer,
so I can whisper where he is.
Now wipe the spit
out of your eyes.

Name:
Mandela of Africa,
I have been here, this island
like a lion in the sea,
a drowning lion;
the sun, the sand,
the rocks to break our backs with –
I have been here how many years,
it is hard to remember,
the years are sun and sand
and rocks to break our hearts with.
Who are you, my brother.
Why are you here.
What do you want.

Children, rotting:
we are old for our years,
we cannot close our eyes,
we are old for our years,
we are bald as old men,
we are bald as babies,
we cannot close our eyes,
we are looking at you,
we are old for our years,
we are looking at you,
we are looking at you,

smiling sadly out of the dusk
of our dying.

Concatenation: An Elegy

"I seek the shop that's full of noise"

Dying, he speaks his childhood's tongue,
Afrikaans of the dusty barefoot dorp
where he lost his heart before his head decayed -
the Jew's daughter's black plaits
friezing above the flyblown counter
in a sibilance of shuffling feet
(the women's eyes flick like lizards' tongues,
their lips jerk in shy rictal grins,
the glistening opulent babies swaddled to their backs
dreaming, dreaming)
while bees groan, horseflies whimper.

"Every phrase and every sentence is an end and a beginning,
Every poem an epitaph"

At last our mouths reach back for words we used
                but never knew,
language of a far country, forgotten, familiar, near.

"An easy commerce of the old and the new"

Poor Clare, I read in the *TLS*,
poor dying John wrote *Don Juan* -
nineteenth-century Borges
ascribble in the dungeon of his mind -
will Byron on the Day of Judgement
giggle, sneer or weep?
Against the windowpane he watches
a spider
unravelling its guts.
"Done nothing," he writes, again, in his diary,
biting his pencil, biting, biting, biting.

"Farewell, a long farewell":
"I, too, take leave of all I ever had"

"It is the blight man was born for"
"as it were, an after-dinner sleep"

Gentle Merrick, in the film I saw last week,
at last lies
gently back, lays
gently down the burden of his life.
"Yea, though I walk through the valley
of the shadow of death ..."
The dwarf cathedral
gently sings a long silence,
elephants trumpet faintly,
gently,
in the hissing grass of the fields of dusk.

    "and whisper to their souls to go" -

    "Do not go gentle into that good night"

    Some like it hot;
    hurt dignity has its devotees;
    and madness its charm.

Gurney in the Great War of his lurching mind.
And Rosenberg playing the Fool in Dead Man's Dump,
    in No Man's Land.
Blunden attended every regimental reunion,
    exit pursued by mouthing memories
    when the ice, at last, cracks.
Brooke - a frail ironic proboscis slits his golden skin.
Sassoon flung bombs at the Boche, his medal to muddy water,
    survived awhile to motor-accidents, marriage and religion.
Thomas gazing at the freckled mud,
    the morning's poppies motionless in mist,
    while the impossible soaring lark
--concussion heaving cacophony flames bursting apocalypse--
And Owen, like a social-worker or a priest, shyly smiles,
    shepherds pityingly his noble sheep
    towards the plunging duckboards.

Black marks on torn pages.
So many ways to die
and one death.

And you too, Anthea,
I wept when I read the letter four hours ago.
"... over the last few months of her illness,
an example of extreme courage.
We shall all miss her."
So I place this
in the centre of my poem,
remembering our last lunch together.
You turn your glass slowly,
we talk of R.C. Hutchinson, of Joyce Cary, Henry Green,
you cannot eat, you sip the dry red wine.

"We ought to pray in our litany for deliverance
from a lingering as well as from a sudden
death. It is not death itself that presents such
terrors to the mind, but dissolution,
and when that begins before death ..."

"*Captain Scott Dead*:
Robert Falcon Scott, Lawrence Oates and three companions
died in February-March 1912,
having reached the South Pole just after Roald Amundsen.
Their bodies and effects were discovered that November
and the episode rapidly became an emblem of self-sacrificial heroism."
Yelp of dying dogs, the snow snarling at the tent,
and one frosted man raised his many bones, and stumbles, and paused,
and turns, and whispered, twitching up his stiff upper lip
"Going out for a leak ... chaps ...
back in a jiffy ... chaps ..."

"Better to go down dignified"

Is that the way?
"Heroism in the abstract" was Roland's ideal.
Ravishing *lingua franca* of our fractured murderous past.

If there is time, if there is a choice -
if there is an audience -
if there is an epic, romance, novel, journal, secretary,
    companion, camera, tape-recorder, poem -

This cat, grey alley-cat,
her head snaking from splayed fur on the slushy street
(Cannon between MacNab and James)
and hissing, hissing, hissing, hissing.
"Pelvis fucked to hell," he mutters,
"cost 300 dollars to fix her up,
have to put her out,"
and he takes her in -
the noosed cat gone unremarkably,
spitting in the swaying SPCA van,
gone to darkness too.

    There is no good way to die.

    There are too many images of death.

    Words like salt-cold salt-smooth salt-burning stones:
    sounds like the sounds of the waves of the sea.

"Bowsprit cracked with ice and paint cracked with heat"
"Oh build your ship of death, for you will need it"
"bones are scattered at the grave's mouth"
"If I should die, think only this of me"
"Just a little white with the dust"
"Time held me green and"
"I am sick, I must die"
"Ripeness is all"
"The years"
"Your"
"I"

        Sounds,
        voices,
        echoes.

"We only live, only suspire,
Consumed by either fire or fire"

The
book
pyramid
weight of words
single-minded he made it
smiling rabbi whose family fed
voracious Auschwitz father wife child
through 40 languages pursuing this marvelous murdering tongue
to its roots in horror horror the horror the shining heart of our darkness
Klein's Comprehensive Etymological Dictionary of the English Language
made for himself love, from death love, beginning and end of the heart

Life

"sitting in a boat, reciting
We perished, each alone,
while he crushes a dying mackerel"

Love

"And join the ranting, roaring boys
To blunt old memory's hornet sting"

Death.

Why Trees?

They leech their lives
from soil and water.
        And so do we.

Flaunt their foliage,
neglect their roots.
        And so do we.

At night they whisper
fury to the stars.
        And so do we.

Over-reaching,
they curse the air,
moan and glare.
They love too late,
and love to hate.
They lie and lie,
and then they die.
        And so do we.

- A nonsense-poem!
Mere skeltonics,
drunk with rhythm,
mad with sound,
and almost free of thought.
Trees alive?
Good God!
One might as well
believe in Hell,
or Global Warming.

Words, Words

I

To write poetry is to put yourself out
like a cat, in the dark.
Stealth requisite, and nerve.
Lust impels fastidious movement
along this narrow wall.
And the ugly shriek.

II

Without the delusion of permanence,
one must still create:
The heart is blind, disturbed,
yearns to shape what's all around
to something understood.
Knowledge is not important.
Belief is not important.
Thought is not important.
But the blind heart –
blind, blind, blindly creating –
the heart is important.

The Golden Spruce

Alone
among trees:
soaring high
above green,
beyond brown.

He cut it down.
He cut it down.

Holy to Haida,
gone:
Great Lion's pelt
food for worms.

And he too,
gone:
the wilderness
has him.

He fought
machines
to save the forest.

They beat him down.
They beat him down.

Shunned, shamed,
he left his kind, he left his world.

Grey,
grey,
grey.
grey.

But when the Spirit of the Golden Spruce
sings again its undefeated holy song, I think, I hope,
he is forgiven, loved, golden.

Acknowledgements

"For John Thompson" was first published in the *Antigonish Review,* Summer–Autumn 1995, pp. 270–272. Quotations in "Pelicans" are from *Macbeth.* "The Golden Spruce" was inspired by John Vaillant's book of the same title (2005).

www.ingramcontent.com/pod-product-compliance
Lightning Source LLC
Chambersburg PA
CBHW020915080526
44589CB00011B/606